Electronic Music and Music Concrète

(*Frontis.*) The author demonstrating electronic and recording equipment at the Dartington Summer School of Music.

F.C. JUDD

Electronic Music and Musique Concrète

Foruli Classics

Foruli Classics

Published by Foruli Classics
First published by Neville Spearman Ltd 1961
This edition published by Foruli Classics 2013
ISBN 978-1-905792-51-1
Cover copyright © Foruli Ltd 2013
Text copyright © F C Judd 1961

The right of Freda Judd to be identified as the owner of the copyright in this work has been asserted by her in accordance with the Copyright, Designs and Patents Act 1988.

All rights reserved. No part of this publication may be reproduced, stored in or introduced into a retrieval system, or transmitted, in any form or by any means (electronic, mechanical, photocopying, recording or otherwise), without the prior written permission of the publisher. This book is sold subject to the condition that it shall not, by way of trade or otherwise, be lent, re-sold, hired out, or otherwise circulated without the publisher's prior written consent in any form of binding or cover other than that in which it is published and without a similar condition including this condition being imposed on the subsequent purchaser.

A CIP catalogue record for this book is available from the British Library

Cover & design by Andy Vella at Velladesign (www.velladesign.com)

Printed by Lightning Source

Foruli Classics is an imprint of Foruli Ltd, London

www.foruliclassics.com

Contents

PART 1 THE ELEMENTS OF ELECTRONIC MUSIC   15

PART 2 ELECTRONIC SOUND SOURCES AND TONE SHAPING   31

PART 3 THE COMPOSITION OF ELECTRONIC MUSIC AND MUSIQUE CONCRÈTE   63

APPENDIX AND NOTES   77

INDEX   89

List of Illustrations

Frontis The Author with electronic equipment at Dartington Hall

facing page 32

Fig: 6 Oscilloscope Display, The Square Wave
Fig: 8 Oscilloscope Display, Modulation
Fig: 9 Oscilloscope Display, Beat Tones

facing page 33

Fig: 11 Play-back machines for the Poem Electronique

between pages 48–49

Fig: 22 Magnetic Pick-ups for Electric Guitar
Fig: 23 Twin neck Electric Guitar
Fig: 25 A Modern Electric Guitar
Fig: 28 Professional tape recorder

between pages 64–65

Fig: 33 Special recording deck for Electronic Music
Fig: 36 Electronic equipment used by the author

facing page 65

Fig: 38 Electronic Music Demonstration at the Centre of Sound

Music is the universal
    language of mankind.
            LONGFELLOW: *Outre-Mer*

PREFACE

The term 'Electronic Music' is sometimes used when compositions, written for conventional musical instruments, are performed with the aid of electronic devices such as the electric organ. In recent years, however, the term has come to mean something quite different, being applied to music whose actual composition is based on the use of electronic aids, especially of magnetic recording. These aids can be employed to create entirely new sounds which neither the electric organ nor any conventional instrument would be capable of producing.

One of the leading figures in this new field of electronic music is the Dutch composer Henk Badings. His Radiophonic opera *Orestes*, in which electronic aids play a substantial part, was awarded the Prix Italia in 1954 and has since received more than 200 performances. In his ballet music *Cain and Abel*, which had its first public performance in May, 1956 at The Hague, he makes almost exclusive use of electronic aids.

In contemporary music various trends of composition have evolved, which may be described under the general heading of 'Electronic Music'. A characteristic common to them all is the use of magnetic recording and other electronic aids for the treatment and transformation of sounds into something entirely new. The composer's 'raw material' may be produced by traditional musical instruments, derived from 'natural sources' (Musique Concrète) or created by electronic means (Ref. 1). These are the *elements* of electronic music which I have attempted to describe in this book, and since it is likely that composer and engineer will work together, I have included a number of basic electronic circuits as well as some notes on the work of other composers.

Acknowledgements are due to the N.V. Phillips Gloeilampenfabrieken, Technical and Scientific Literature Department, Eindhoven, the Netherlands, for permission to include details of the production of the electronic music of the *Cain and Abel* ballet, the *Electronic Poem* and the photographs illustrating these works.

South Woodford, 1961   F.C.J.

PART ONE

The Elements of Electronic Music

The Elements of Electronic Music

Electronic engineering enters into the creation of Electronic Music and Musique Concrète in several ways. It provides new sources of sound and makes it possible to manipulate and transform sound and finally control the reproduction of the music. The term 'Electronic Reproduction' implies the re-creation by means of amplifiers and loudspeakers of sound originally created at another place or at another time.

The appreciation of every type of reproduction is primarily determined by the criterion of its fidelity to the original and the familiar shortcomings of electronic reproduction in this respect, i.e. noise, distortion and the 'hole-in-the-wall' effect of single loudspeakers can be eliminated to some extent by improvement, for example, in electronic circuits and in recording methods (magnetic recording) and by the introduction of the stereophonic technique. Here resides the freedom with which a sound source or sources can be arranged within a given space.

Electronic reproduction offers numerous possibilities of practical importance, most of which lie in the electronic circuits of the apparatus. For example, where the component sound signal is available in a form by which the strength (volume) can be controlled by the extremely simple expedient of turning a potentiometer knob. Volume control, and with it the mixing of different parts of tone patterns in any desired proportion, is a well-established practice in broadcasting studios. With a volume control one can introduce dynamic figures in tones or combinations of tones where this would otherwise be impossible, as, for example, in a dying piano chord. By a rapid movement of the volume control a note struck on a percussion instrument can be deprived of its 'attack', thus giving a pianoforte chord, for example, a rather unique character.

Magnetic tape is also a most important aid to the creation of electronic music, not only because of the wide scope it offers for the transformation of a sound, but because it was with this medium that it first became possible to register individual sounds, transform them, and put them together again as a unified whole. In other words, to compose them in the musical sense.

The manipulation of magnetic tape is not the only method of transforming sounds. An obvious method is to use electrical networks with which variable linear distortion can be effected by sharp or gradual cut-off beyond which the sound is attentuated or even suppressed; by this means a particular narrow range of frequencies in each note can be given a dominant significance (creation of formants).

Another sound-transforming device is the ring-

The Elements of Electronic Music 17

modulator of the type used in carrier-wave telephony. The modulator is arranged to have two equivalent pairs of input terminals and if two musical tones are applied to these terminals both tones appear at the output, together with all their combination tones (intermodulation products). Of these, the difference tone (beat frequency) is the most prominent. If one input signal is a musical chord and the other a pure sine wave, the chord will appear at the output, accompanied by a shadow chord.

By the manipulation of magnetic tape quite new sounds can be produced and made audible via the loudspeaker; they are therefore effectively 'original' sounds although they were never picked up by a microphone. Once familiar with this idea, it soon becomes obvious that we can dispense entirely with the primary sound that would normally be picked up by a microphone.

An excellent example of electronic music produced by the manipulation of magnetic tape and various electronic sound sources is the composition of *Cain and Abel* by Badings; a recording issued by Philips Limited of Eindhoven.

SOUND SOURCES

The simplest electronic sound source available is the *sine-wave generator*. A loudspeaker connected to such an instrument delivers an almost purely sinusoidal sound pressure, that is, a tone practically devoid of harmonics and which sounds strange and ethereal.

The pitch of the tone can be continuously varied by turning the frequency control, and by this method glissandi (gliding tone) can be produced at will. Its greatest virtue, however, is that it does offer a simple means of obtaining accurate notes with various intervals, i.e. any desired scale. One could, therefore, deliberately depart from the conventional equal temperament scale which divides the octave into twelve equal intervals. In the *Cain and Abel* recording mentioned above, repeated use is made of pure harmonic intervals, that is to say intervals exactly equal to the whole-numbered frequency ratios of the harmonic series. Although these intervals sound somewhat unusual they can eventually be accepted by the ear as being melodious.

The counterpart of the sine-wave generator is another familiar electronic device which is widely used for time-base and counting systems, i.e. the *multi-vibrator*. This produces a sound which contains a large number of harmonics, which differ in intensity according to some slowly varying function. The resulting signal, which may have a square or sawtooth waveform, can be further modified by passing it through an electrical filter or 'shaping' circuit.

Another sound source is the *Noise Generator*, and this device differs from all other known sources in that the sound it produces has a continuous spectrum. Noise having a constant energy distribution over the entire spectrum of audible frequencies is, musically, not particularly interesting, since nothing can be varied except its intensity. This type of noise, sometimes called 'white noise', can, however, be filtered into bands having a definite pitch and an unusual timbre.

In the electronic sound sources so far mentioned the frequencies of the vibrations, with all their components, are determined by electrical elements. In another, rather hybrid group of electronic sound sources, the frequencies are determined by mechanical means, although the vibrations only become acoustically effective through the medium of a loudspeaker. Two kinds belonging to this group were used in the production of the Philips *Cain and Abel* recording. These were the 'Electronic Drums' and an 'Electronic Clavichord'. One of the drums was essentially a large condenser microphone whose vibrations were produced by taps or drum rolls on the diaphragm whilst the second drum consisted of a steel sheet, the vibrations being picked up at a specific position by a piezo-electric crystal.

One other source of electronic sound may be of interest. This is an optical siren, and in this device the pitch is determined mechanically by the speed of a motor-driven disc, the tone itself being produced by optical means. The tone pattern is cut out in a sheet of paper and successively scanned by apertures in the revolving disc which interrupts a beam of light. The light variation so produced is converted into electrical current variations by a photo-electric cell.

ANALYSIS OF SOUND WAVES

When considering the production of audible sound waves by electronic methods it becomes necessary to have some understanding of oscillation and the analysis of complex waveforms. The scientists Hemholtz and Fourier have proved mathematically that any waveform, no matter how complex, may be resolved into individual frequency components. Therefore frequency as well as amplitude and harmonic content can be calculated. It is not necessary here to delve into complex mathematics, however, and accordingly more simple explanations and some practical examples will be given.

The pitch of a fundamental wave determines the period of time within which all other associated waves must be present. Fig. 1 represents a sine wave such as that produced from a tuning fork, or a sine-wave generator. The sine wave is the simplest form of recurrent wave and does, in fact, represent a simple harmonic motion which can be seen with the aid of an electronic measuring instrument called an oscilloscope.

The form or shape of any sound or electric wave may, however, be illustrated conveniently for the purpose of analysis, as in Fig. 1, which shows that the amplitude of a wave is the height of a peak from the axis whilst the period is the time for one complete curve. The *frequency* is the number of complete curves in a given unit of time, usually seconds. The velocity of a wave is its wavelength times the number of waves per second.

The energy of intensity (E) of a sine wave varies as the square of the amplitude (a) with constant frequency (f) and as the square of the frequency with constant amplitude. If both amplitude and frequency vary, the intensity varies as the square of the product of amplitude and frequency ($E = f^2 \times a^2$). (Ref. 2.)

In order to illustrate the complete waveform of a complex sound, a simple drawing could be given, although an analysis of a number of cycles might show that the different frequency components were not necessarily in the same phase. Such an analysis could of course be made directly with an oscilloscope. Reference to the drawing of a simple sine wave (Fig. 1) will show that one complete cycle of operations extends from 0 to 1. Within this cycle will also be the harmonics which may be present if we are dealing with a 'complex' sound wave. The effect of adding the second harmonic, which is one octave higher, is shown in Fig. 2. The original sine wave,

The Elements of Electronic Music

shown as a dotted curve, is changed in shape and because of the addition of the second harmonic will now assume an appearance shown by the solid line. The complete wave is no longer symmetrical along the time base because the addition of the second harmonic has caused the centre of the wave to move slightly to the left.

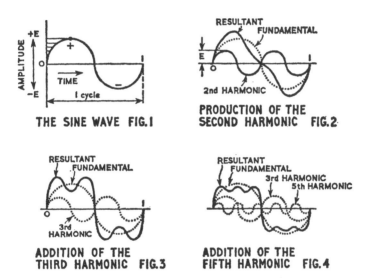

THE SINE WAVE FIG.1

PRODUCTION OF THE SECOND HARMONIC FIG.2

ADDITION OF THE THIRD HARMONIC FIG.3

ADDITION OF THE FIFTH HARMONIC FIG.4

If a third harmonic only is added to a sine wave the effect will be as shown in Fig. 3, from which it may be seen that the composite wave is now symmetrical in each half because the third harmonic has a node at this point. The effect of adding a fifth harmonic will be seen from Fig. 4.

If the frequency difference between two waves were very great the effect of mixing is like that shown by the diagram of Fig. 5 where the waveform resulting from the addition of a fundamental frequency and another frequency of a ratio approximately 4½ to 1 has been used as an illustration.

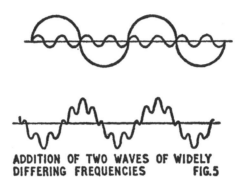

ADDITION OF TWO WAVES OF WIDELY DIFFERING FREQUENCIES   FIG.5

A transient sound contains a large number of harmonics and if sustained for a time would appear on an oscilloscope, as shown by Fig. 6. Such a wave is usually referred to as a *square wave* and its special property is such that it contains only odd harmonics in addition to the fundamental. The square wave is extremely useful for the production of electronic music as the audible tone is rich, chiefly because of the large number of harmonics.

The sawtooth wave contains both odd and even harmonics up to at least the 30th and its analysis from the individual sine-wave components as shown in Fig. 7. Most sounds, whether musical or not, are composed of complex waveforms and speech is one of the most complicated. To give some idea of this, the photograph of Fig. 8 has been included, and shows an oscilloscope display of the spoken sound of 'AH' which is modulatnig a radio-frequency carrier.

The Elements of Electronic Music

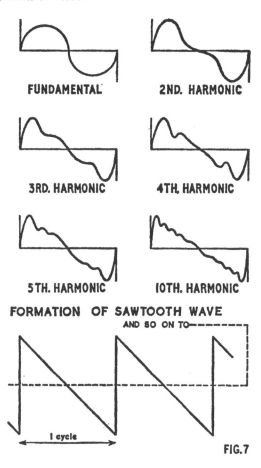

FIG. 7

BEAT NOTES

Another very important characteristic of sound waves which applies to electronically generated tones as well as to those produced acoustically is an effect due to oscillations sounding simultaneously and of nearly, but not quite, the same pitch. If two such notes sound together, the one of higher pitch may complete a cycle before the lower-pitched one. The respective frequencies add at one moment, are equal at another, and in opposition to each other at yet another instance.

This gives rise to an undulating sound, at a new frequency, which is called a 'beat note'. The beat note frequency will be $f_b = f^1 - f^2$ where f^1 and f^2 are the two mixed frequencies. The photograph of Fig. 9 shows the formation of one of these notes.

Beat notes can have a pleasing or displeasing effect, displeasure being generally experienced when the number of beats are comparable with the frequency of the fundamental tone. Beat tones do in fact contribute much more to music than is generally realised; for example, the ear will often detect a strong fundamental tone in the lower notes of a violin when in fact the real fundamental of the same pitch is weak. Strong upper harmonics usually adjacent to each other produce beat notes which sometimes sound like a fundamental.

Beat notes are often introduced into an otherwise steady tone to produce a tremolo or vibrato effect. Such beat notes are usually of very low frequency, and as the frequency differences involved are great the main tone becomes modulated and has an audibly distinguishable wavering which is often regarded as essential, especially in natural voice music.

Whilst the formation of beat notes will provide richness to individual musical instruments and to artificially generated tones, it must be made clear that any amplifiers used for the overall amplification of tones or electronic musical instruments must be carefully designed so as to *prevent* the formation of beat notes. This is in fact a design requirement for any high-fidelity amplifier.

PRODUCING ELECTRICAL TONES

There are a number of methods by which tones can be produced electronically, the most common being electronic tone generators or oscillators.

The well-known 'sine-wave generator' or 'audio oscillator' normally used for testing amplifiers is one example of a device from which pure sinusoidal waves of varying frequency may be obtained. An electronic valve will generate a continuous wave if part of the output voltage is fed back into the input circuit in order to maintain oscillation. If sufficient voltage is fed back, the oscillation will build up indefinitely, although the amplitude of the oscillation will be limited by the characteristic of the valve. This implies the possibility of a distorted waveform, but with careful design a sine-wave oscillator can be made to provide a purely sinusoidal output with a harmonic content of less than 1 per cent of the fundamental. One example of a good sine-wave oscillator is shown as the circuit of Fig. 10 and which is known as a *phase-shift* oscillator. The circuit is very stable

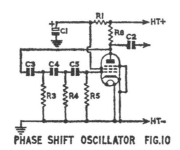

PHASE SHIFT OSCILLATOR FIG.10

TYPICAL COMPONENT VALUES
*C1 — 8mfd. C2 — 0·1mfd.
C3, c4, C5 — 0·001mfd. R3, R4, R5 — 470K.ohm.
R8 — 10K.ohm. R1 — 47K.ohm.*

and is often used for vibrato control in electronic organs and in conjunction with amplifiers for other electric musical instruments such as the electric guitar.

A more commonly used oscillator is one which generates square waves which are consequently rich in harmonics extending to very high frequencies. The square-wave generator is generally used as the basis for small electronic organs because the square waveform can be 'shaped' to provide tones with different harmonic content. A single oscillator can be made to provide a very wide range of frequencies but it should be appreciated that only one note can be selected at a time. Commercially produced instruments, such as the 'Solovox' and the 'Clavioline', are good examples of simple electronic musical instruments which use square-wave oscillators. A full-range organ usually has a large number of valve oscillators or other type of tone generator, very often using one for each note of the instrument.

Three other methods of producing sounds electrically must be appended to those already mentioned above. These are listed as follows:

1. The Noise Generator
2. Optical-Electrical methods (tone patterns).
3. Electro-magnetic pick-ups.

The optical-electrical method has already been mentioned and further information concerning the noise generator will be given later. One of the *electro-magnetic* methods is that of reproducing the sound of steel strings such as those of the guitar, piano, banjo, etc., by means of a 'magnetic pick-up'. The term 'pick-up' although commonly used, is not entirely correct, since the vibration of the steel strings is merely used to disturb a magnetic field surrounding a coil, thus producing electric currents in the coil. However, the method may be used very effectively for direct reproduction over a loudspeaker and since an amplifier must be used in conjunction with this method, the tone quality may be changed and electronically controlled effects introduced.

When any of the sounds from the sources that have been mentioned are reproduced via the medium of magnetic tape, a very great measure of control is possible. With the additional application of purely electronic control, the range of new sounds and effects are almost unlimited.

Equally remarkable effects can be obtained with the technique of *stereophony;* sounds can be made to issue from a direction where there is no sound source and by means of electronic manipulation the impression of a moving sound can be created without there being any actual movement of the source. These effects were considered, when at the end of 1956, the Philips Company of Holland discussed the sound effects for the *Electronic Poem* with Architect M. Le Corbusier. It was required that the audience should have the illusion that various sounds were in motion around them, rising and falling, coming together and moving apart again. It was also decided that the space in which this took place was to seem 'narrow and dry' at one instance, and at another to have the reverberation of a cathedral. The final reproduction of the electronic music that was composed by Edgar Varese was obtained from a three-track tape recording, the whole system being controlled by a second magnetic tape containing no fewer than fifteen tracks (Fig. 11) (Ref. 3).

We have so far dealt only with electronic methods of producing sounds which themselves could be used for the composition of actual music on some theme such as the

Cain and Abel ballet mentioned earlier. Simpler methods of producing sounds via an electronic medium are possible, and since these are within the scope of the musician they will accordingly be described. The methods are those which employ magnetic or crystal pick-ups in conjunction with certain existing types of musical instruments. This is of course almost similar to using a microphone but does, however, provide a method of recording without natural reverberation and a means whereby the sound from the instrument can be greatly amplified.

MAGNETIC AND CRYSTAL PICK-UP UNITS

The magnetic pick-up is used mainly for those instruments employing steel strings such as the Plectrum Guitar, the Mandolin and the Pianoforte.

Contact pick-ups of the crystal type are really low-sensitivity microphones but are useful for direct attachment to almost any musical instrument. This type of pick-up is popular with dance band musicians for amplifying the weaker-sounding instruments.

The plectrum electric guitar lends itself readily to direct tape recording and electronic treatment, and one has only to listen to some of the 'pop records' featuring these instruments in order to realise the possibilities. An excellent example of the multiple-tape recording and electronic-treatment techniques are those used by Les Paul. This versatile guitarist employs multi-channel recording equipment which enables him to feature 'several' guitars, giving the combined sound of a small orchestra. He also uses different recording speeds for the production of rapid arpeggios.

PART TWO
Electronic Sound Sources and Tone Shaping

Electronic Sound Sources and Tone Shaping

THE MULTI-VIBRATOR AS A TONE SOURCE

Often used as a primary tone source for an electronic organ, the multi-vibrator basic circuit is shown as Fig. 12. With suitable circuit constants a range of at least three octaves of continuously variable or 'keyed' tones can be obtained and the construction of such a device is not difficult. For experimental work an arrangement with simple wire keys is quite suitable.

The basic circuit shows that two valves are used and these may, in fact, be a conventional 'double triode'. The multi-vibrator is a self-generating oscillator, but one which can be stopped or started instantaneously, thus making it eminently suitable for keying. The circuit oscillates readily and is not critical in design or operation. It can be locked to an injected frequency and the amplitude of the output voltage may be varied slowly or rapidly by means of an applied sinusoidal voltage from a separate oscillator (vibrato).

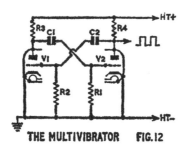

TYPICAL COMPONENT VALUES
$C1, C2 - 0{\cdot}001mfd$
$R1, R2 - 470K.ohm.$
$R3, R4 - 47K.ohm.$

THE MULTIVIBRATOR   FIG. 12

The principle of operation is very briefly described as follows. The multi-vibrator is essentially a two-valve resistance/capacitance coupled amplifier in which the whole of the output of V2 is fed back to the grid of V1 so that the circuit oscillates violently, the oscillation being such that the valves are alternately completely cut off or conducting with the grids somewhat positive. Its principal properties are that voltage and current wave-forms are almost square and therefore very rich in harmonics. The frequency of the oscillation can be controlled by the 'time constants' of the circuit (C1, R1 and C2, R2) and if necessary synchronised by an injected signal. (Because of this property the M/V is used for frequency dividing and counting in special electronic devices.) (Ref. 4.)

COMPLETE CIRCUIT FOR THE PRODUCTION OF TONES

A useful circuit which will serve as the basis for experiment or for the construction of a more complete unit is shown in circuit form as Fig. 13. This is a simple twin

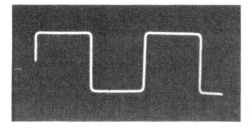

Fig. 6. A Square-wave as displayed by an oscilloscope.

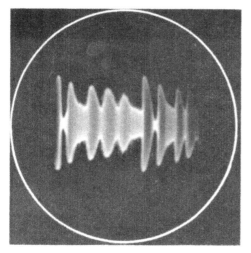

Fig. 8. Modulation by the spoken word 'ah' (from an oscilloscope display).

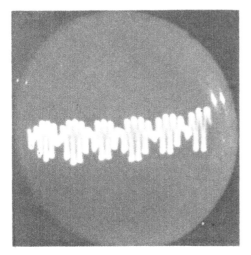

Fig. 9. Beat tones produced by Ring Modulation (oscilloscope display).

Fig. 11. Special play-back machines for the three-track tape carrying the electronic music by Varèse and for the fifteen-track control tape. Two of the four machines were used for the performance of the 'Electronic Poem' in the Philips Pavilion at the 1958 Brussels World Fair.

Electronic Sound Sources and Tone Shaping 33

triode multi-vibrator covering about three octaves and includes a 'vibrato' oscillator. The initial 'pitch' is set by the potentiometer R1 and each subsequent semi-tone downwards is adjusted by VR2, VR3, VR4, etc., to the limit of the octave range as determined by C1, C2 or C3. The resistor values for each semi-tone will be a little in excess of 1,000 ohms per step, so it is advisable to use variables (VR2, VR3, etc.) each with a total value of about 2,000 ohms.

The pitch can be shifted up or down an octave by switching the capacitors C1, C2, C3, each of which should be paralleled by a low-value trimmer-type capacitor. These are for setting the pitch of each octave relative to the other. The first part of the circuit V1a,

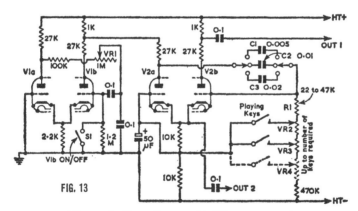

Electronic Tone Source with Vibratto control.

V2b is another M/V circuit which provides a continuously variable low-frequency oscillation for vibrato effect. This is switched on or off by S1 and the rate of oscillation, between about 5 and 10 c.p.s. is controlled by the potentiometer VR1.

2—EM

The tone oscillator must work into a buffer valve and from there on may be coupled directly to an amplifier for direct reproduction over a loud speaker or into a tape-recording amplifier high-level input. (Fig. 14.) A pre-set volume control has been added to the circuit so that the output may be adjusted for correct recording level.

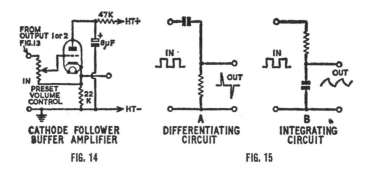

CATHODE FOLLOWER BUFFER AMPLIFIER
FIG. 14

A DIFFERENTIATING CIRCUIT

B INTEGRATING CIRCUIT

FIG. 15

TONE SHAPING

Tone-forming networks may be included to give a variety of pleasing tones and effects. Of these the most simple are the 'differentiating' and 'integrating' networks and the inductive type filters, all of which are capable of producing a wide range of tone colours. A carefully designed inductive filter can be used to eliminate harmonics almost entirely so that a square wave could, in fact, be converted to an almost pure sine wave (Ref. 2).

The tone-forming networks mentioned above, however, will provide enough variation to satisfy most requirements and these are shown, together with the wave forms that can be derived from a square-wave input.

Electronic Sound Sources and Tone Shaping

Fig. 15A shows the differentiating circuit and the resultant sound which is high pitched and thin but not unpleasant when accompanied by rounder and deeper tones.

The integrating circuit produces a nearly sawtooth wave, this having a distinctive tone, rather more round than the fundamental square wave but less ethereal than a pure sine wave (Fig. 15B). The circuit of Fig. 16 shows a complete yet simple and effective tone-shaping arrangement, which may follow the basic electronic tone generating circuit of Fig. 13.

These devices will provide at least three octaves of infinitely variable tones; the equivalent of a small orchestra of instruments, particularly if they are used in conjunction with magnetic tape manipulation and other transformation methods to be described later.

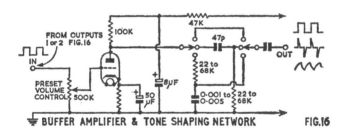
BUFFER AMPLIFIER & TONE SHAPING NETWORK   FIG.16

THE SINE-WAVE OSCILLATOR

Mentioned in earlier paragraphs, the sine wave is devoid of harmonics and sounds weird and mournful when compared with the richer tones from a square-wave generator. Circuits for a continuously variable or keyed range pure-tone oscillator are rather specialised and consequently require a more intimate knowledge of oscillator fundamentals and design. A ready-made continuously variable sine wave source covering more than the audible frequency range is the *audio signal generator* of the type used by service engineers and laboratory technicians for testing low-frequency amplifiers. Alternatively a standard 33 r.p.m. frequency test record* is a useful substitute and has been used by the author as a pure tone source for electronic music.

NOISE GENERATOR

A simple noise generator can be devised from a single-valve super-regenerative oscillator, which because of its peculiar circuit operation produces a high-pitched continuous hiss. When suitably keyed, bursts of noise rather similar to the sound of a struck cymbal but without the familiar 'attack' can be obtained; noise of this nature was used to obtain the electronically produced sound of cymbals in the *Cain and Abel* recording mentioned earlier. The circuit of Fig. 17 will work quite readily and has an output sufficient for most purposes. It may be used in conjunction with one of the 'gating' or keying circuits described later. The pitch of the noise may be altered by adjustment of the trimmer capacitor

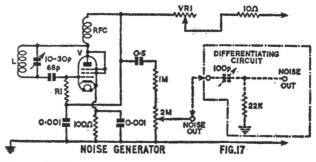

* Decca LXT.5346.

Electronic Sound Sources and Tone Shaping 37

C1 and the quench control VR1, which should have a value of about 50,000 ohms. If an audible high-pitched whistle is produced as well as the noise or hiss, it may be necessary to adjust VR1 in conjunction with C1 to get rid of the whistle. The grid leak R1 is also critical in this respect but should have a value between 3·3 and 10 M.ohms. This inductance L may consist of ten turns of 18 s.w.g. enamelled or tinned copper-wire wound into a coil approximately one inch long and half an inch in diameter with spacing between turns of a little less than the thickness of each turn. The choke (RFC) may be a standard radio receiver type (see appendix).

The additional circuit shown in dotted lines will be found useful for obtaining a higher-pitched source of noise produced by the differentiating characteristics of the 100 pfd. variable capacitor and the 22K variable resistor. It should be connected as indicated, but the use of this circuit will somewhat reduce the voltage output otherwise obtainable.

Filtered 'white noise' may also be obtained, pre-recorded on magnetic tape. It is recorded in one-third octave bands covering almost the entire audio frequency range (Ref. 14. Appendix).

GATING CIRCUITS

In order to produce specific kinds of sound from basic tones, such as those of the sine-wave or square-wave generator, it may be necessary to provide artificial attack and/or decay. On the other hand the composer may wish to deprive a sound of its attack or decay. The automatic 'bell-gate' of Fig. 18 may be used to great effect when it is desired to remove 'attack' and then allow sound to decay gradually. Both the 'starting up'

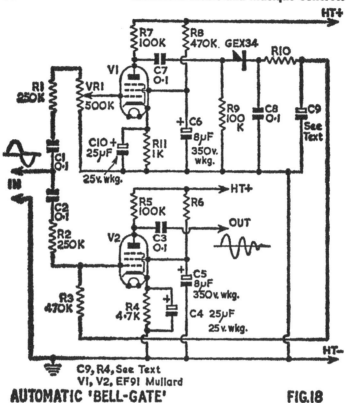

AUTOMATIC 'BELL-GATE' FIG.18

and the decay times may be controlled so that sounds may be given a pizzicato effect.

The keyed or controlled bell-gate (Fig. 19) is useful for providing the sounds of bells, for example, from a continuously running oscillator. The fundamental tone is fed into the gating circuit but no signal will be passed until the gate is opened or keyed by the switch S1. The attack produced is similar to that of a struck bell and the decay time may be controlled by the setting of VR1. The circuit may also be used for short but

Electronic Sound Sources and Tone Shaping 39

decaying bursts of noise from the noise generator (Fig. 17) which when mixed with a tone fairly rich in harmonics (also passed through the gate) produces a sound similar to that of a struck cymbal.

(Circuit details) *Controlled Bell-Gate*. Any medium-impedance triode valve will be suitable. S1, the keying switch, should have a quick make-and-break action. *Automatic Bell-Gate*. The action of this circuit is briefly as follows: V2 is cut off by cathode bias determined by the value of R4 which for an EF91 valve will be about 4·7 K.ohms. The input signal is applied to the grids of both valves but through a gain control to the grid of V1. The positive going rectified output from V1 will lift the grid of V2 so that this valve conducts when a signal is applied at the input terminal. When the signal ceases V2 will gradually be returned to cut off as the charge on the capacitor C9 decreases. The value of C9, which should be averagely about 1 mfd., may be modified accordingly.

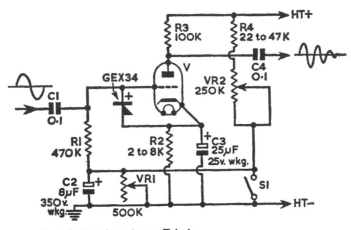

V Medium Impedance Triode
S1 Keying Switch, spring loaded (micro-switch)

CONTROLLED 'BELL-GATE'   **FIG.19**

40 Electronic Music and Musique Concrète

An earlier paragraph mentioned the use of the volume control for producing effects similar to those described above. Whilst the rapid turning of a volume control can deprive a tone or sound of its attack, the method is rather cumbersome in cases where it is desired to control a rapid succession of notes, such as can be achieved with a gating circuit.

OTHER SOUND SOURCES

The drums and gongs circuit of Fig. 20 requires rather more knowledge and experience of electronics generally. However, the basic circuit is similar to that used for condenser microphones and the principle of operation is the same. The metal plates are set very closely together but are insulated from each other. This forms a capacity between the grid of the amplifier valve V1 and the h.t. rail. The capacitor (two plates) will become charged via R2 and any change in the capacity set up by the two plates will result in a varying potential at the

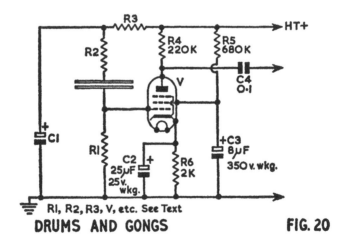

DRUMS AND GONGS   FIG. 20

Electronic Sound Sources and Tone Shaping

grid of the valve. A change in capacity would therefore be made by striking one of the plates. The rate of change of capacitance will be that of the resonant frequency of the plate being struck.

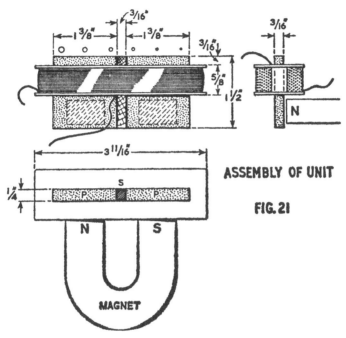

ASSEMBLY OF UNIT

FIG. 21

CONSTRUCTIONAL DETAILS FOR A MAGNETIC PICK-UP

For a high impedance input a total of 4,400 turns of 36 swg. enamelled copper wire will be required.
The Pole Pieces (P) should be cut from mild steel. The spacer (S) between them may be hard wood or bakelite. U-shaped magnets can be obtained from surplus dealers. The pole pieces may require a small amount of packing in order to secure them firmly in the paxolin bobbin.

The Plectrum Electric Guitar

Nearly all modern electric guitars feature the magnetic pick-up, which is usually fitted just beneath the steel strings of the instrument. Fig. 21 shows the general arrangement required for a magnetic pick-up suitable for a plectrum or Hawaiian-type guitar. The photograph (Fig. 22) shows one position for a pick-up unit, which in this case is at the end of the finger-board where it will provide a fairly deep, mellow tone. The guitar in the photograph features two pick-ups, the second one being constructed as a bridge *over* the strings. In this position the tone obtained is rather sharp and hard. Both units are fed into a 'fader' control so that the player my change from one unit to the other, so having a selection of two different tones.

Also in the photograph can be seen a *damping control* which is operated from the lever visible at the waist of the instrument. Damping is effected by means of a felt pad which comes down on to the strings very close to the bridge.

Guitar pick-ups may be purchased from almost any musical instrument dealer. Most of these pick-ups are high impedance and therefore suitable for direct connection to the grid circuit of an amplifier. The output is considerably greater than that obtainable from a very sensitive crystal microphone.

The Hawaiian Electric Guitar

An Electric Hawaiian Guitar is not difficult to construct, although hard wood, absolutely straight and free from warps, should be used. The pick-up heads may be constructed like the one in Fig. 21 or commercially made heads may be used. The frets on the guitar shown in the photograph Fig. 23 were cut from $\frac{1}{16}$th in. brass strip set into the finger board to a depth of $\frac{1}{4}$ in. The bridge and nut should be made from brass or steel and be

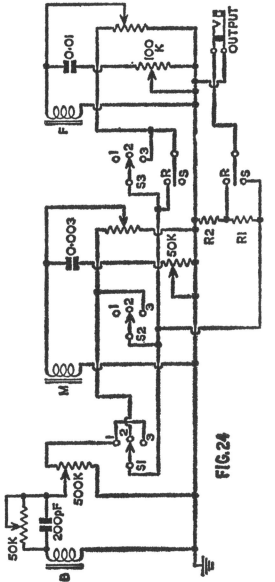

CIRCUIT FOR THE CONTROL UNIT OF AN ELECTRIC GUITAR EMPLOYING THREE MAGNETIC PICK-UPS (B, M, F:—The pick-ups are placed at the 'bridge', 'middle' and 'finger-board' respectively).

high enough to allow approximately $\frac{1}{2}$ in. clearance between the frets and the strings. The distance between the bridge and the nut should be sufficient to allow for not less than twenty-two frets. These instruments may be constructed for six or seven strings, and by using a twin instrument like the one shown in the photograph two different tunings are available, thus increasing the range of chords and scales (Ref. 5).

This guitar lends itself very readily for making multiple recordings and as a sound source for electronic music. One of the main features of the Hawaiian instrument is the unusual glissandi effects that can be produced.

For those who are interested in the construction of an electric guitar with more than one 'pick-up', the 'control' circuit of Fig. 24 provides for musical tone and volume control as well as the selection of one, two or three magnetic pick-ups. The controls may be arranged on the body of the instrument as shown in the photograph of Fig. 25.

This circuit provides for a wide range of tonal effects; for example, a pick-up mounted very close to the bridge will give a 'sharp' tone due to the greater strength of harmonics at that point.

Crystal Pick-ups and other Musical Instruments

Little more can be said about the use of the crystal pick-up or 'contact microphone' except that one could be fitted to almost any musical instrument and connected directly to a recording amplifier. These units are small and light enough to be held on to the instrument with an elastic band or 'Sellotape'. Experiments should be carried out to ascertain the optimum position for these devices as resonance in the body of the instrument may cause unpleasant accentuation of certain notes.

Electronic Vibraphone

An electronic vibraphone using steel bars for the notes could be constructed using a system of electro-magnetic pick-ups as for the electric guitar. Such a device produces clear tones, the impact tone practically disappearing when the sound is amplified. Vibrato may be applied to the amplifier by one of the methods described in earlier paragraphs (Ref. 2).

Tone-correcting Network

A useful tone-correcting network of the passive type is shown as Fig. 26A together with the response curve, Fig. 26B obtainable with this form of network. It should be remembered, however, that the circuit will considerably attenuate signals fed into it so that additional amplification may be required to restore the input signal to its original level.

THE RING-MODULATOR

This is a device frequently employed in electronic music creation, but is, however, an expensive one and very difficult to obtain. Audio-frequency ring-modulators are used in carrier telephony applications, and for these and other specialised purposes the modulator must be perfectly balanced. As a consequence it employs specially designed and therefore expensive transformers. For electronic music purposes one is only concerned with the actual modulation of one tone by another and a reasonably balanced ring-modulator will suffice.

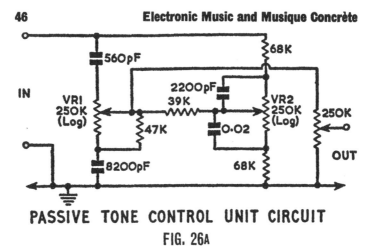

PASSIVE TONE CONTROL UNIT CIRCUIT
FIG. 26A

It will be seen from the circuit of Fig. 27 that two input terminals are provided. In use, a tone is fed into each input, and because of the rectifiers and the special function of the circuit one tone will be modulated by the other and as a consequence new tones will be produced at other frequencies. The audible effect is rather peculiar and is demonstrated in the author's recording 'Experiment in Sound' (Ref. 16).

A simple but effective ring-modulator can be constructed from two audio-frequency intervalve transformers with centre-tapped primary or secondary windings and four germanium diodes (X1, X2, X3 and X4). The circuit of Fig. 27 will not allow complete balance, although this is not necessary, but attenuators should be provided as shown to control the level of the input signals, otherwise distortion will occur.

There are of course many other electronic devices used in electronic music and Musique Concrète production; most are too complex for even the knowledgeable amateur to construct and in any case require elaborate testing

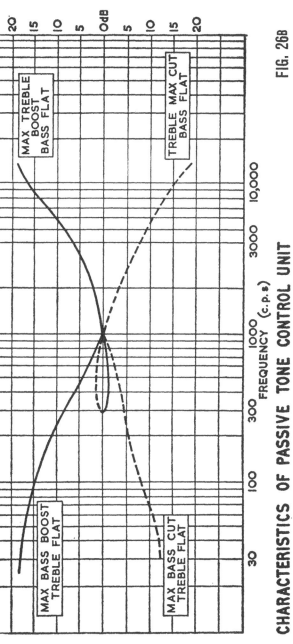

FIG. 26B CHARACTERISTICS OF PASSIVE TONE CONTROL UNIT

instruments in order to check their respective functions. (I have attempted to provide as much information as possible for the technically minded, but to go further would mean assuming a readership of electronic engineers, for the processes that can and are being used would only be fully understood by them.) (Author's note.)

SIMPLE RECORDING TECHNIQUES

Not all tape recorders permit track-to-track multiple recording techniques, but two or more machines can be used most effectively, the procedure being to record first on one machine and then transfer the recording, with added materials, to the other machine (Ref. 16).

Remember also that a recording already on a tape may become distorted by re-recording unless proper precautions are taken. It is essential too that no 'noise' is gathered during recording and re-recording processes, and for professional work only the highest-grade recording and amplifying equipment must be used (Fig. 28). Such equipment is extremely expensive and many of the auxiliary electronic devices used for electronic and concrete music composition may have to be specially made. A ring-modulator, for example, is not an item that one can purchase readily from an electronics manufacturer or dealer. Special filters, too, are very costly and would normally have to be designed and constructed for this particular application. This is one reason why an electronic music studio, where composers can work with the best equipment, is badly needed in Great Britain.

ARTIFICIAL REVERBERATION

For artificial reverberation an amplifier may be used in conjunction with an extra replay head fitted to the tape

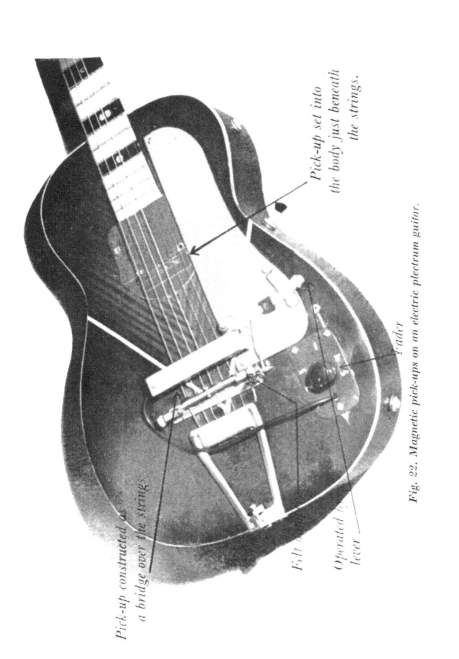

Fig. 22. *Magnetic pick-ups on an electric plectrum guitar.*

Fig. 23. A twin neck electric Hawaiian Guitar.

Fig. 25. A modern electric plectrum guitar with three magnetic pick-ups, Tone controls and Volume controls.

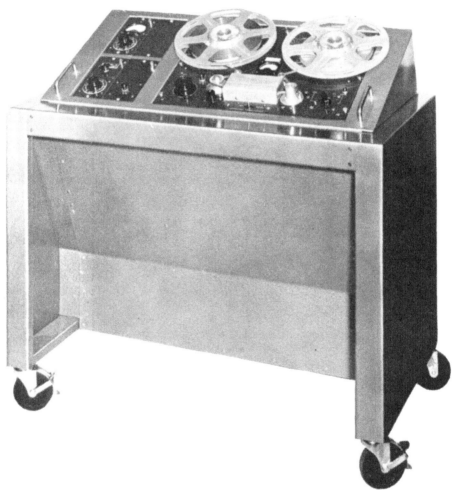

Fig. 28. *Professional Tape Recorder (photo by courtesy of Leevers Rich Ltd.)*

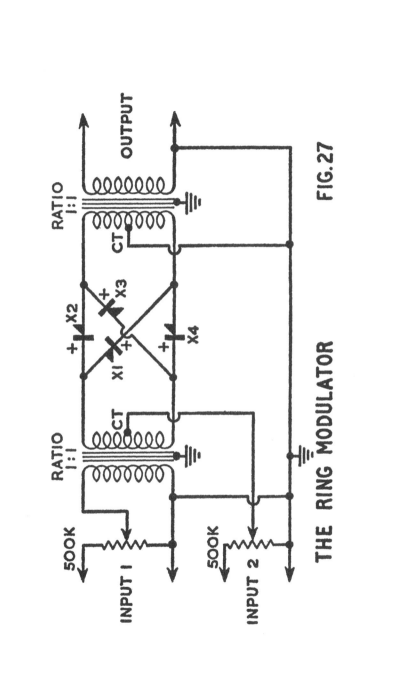

FIG. 27 THE RING MODULATOR

recorder. Those readers who feel inclined to modify a domestic recorder will find that the amplifier circuit of Fig. 29 is suitable for tape head pre-amplification since it incorporates a switched bass correction circuit. Alternatively it may be used as straight microphone pre-amplifier in conjunction with a simple resistive mixer circuit.

The amplifier uses a Mullard EF86 low-noise valve and when switched for tape replay provides about 25 dB bass lift at 50 c.p.s. This is close enough to the C.C.I.R. pre-emphasis characteristic required for tape playback. Very few components are needed and the pre-amplifier will operate from a small power supply or from an h.t.–l.t. supply socket which is provided on some tape recorders. Current consumption at 200–250 v. h.t. is little more than 1 milli-amp and l.t. consumption at 6·3 v. is 0·3 amps.

With the changeover switch in position 2 (mic) the EF86 will operate at full gain with an input impedance suitable for crystal microphones, with the switch in position 2 (tape head) the overall gain of the amplifier is reduced because of the bass pre-emphasis requirement for tape playback. There should be enough output voltage, however, to load the radio or pick-up socket of a recorder.

Operated as a tape head pre-amplifier the circuit of Fig. 29 can be adapted for direct monitoring of a recording from any machine fitted with an extra replay head, placed *after* the regular tape head. The diagram of Fig. 30 will help to clarify the arrangement.

A similar system can be used for producing echoes but most recorders will require a mixing circuit unless provision is already made on the recorder for mixing microphone or radio or pick-up. Fig. 31 shows the basic arrangement and the path of the signal after it has been picked off from the tape. A volume control must be included in the circuit between the tape head and the

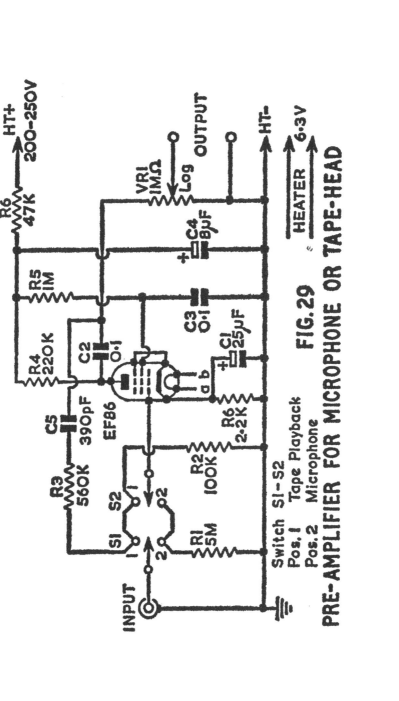

FIG.29 PRE-AMPLIFIER FOR MICROPHONE OR TAPE-HEAD

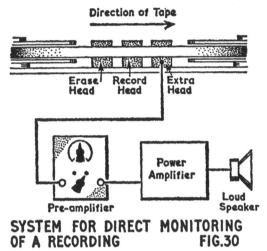

SYSTEM FOR DIRECT MONITORING OF A RECORDING   FIG.30

recording amplifier. This is provided for in the preamplifier, which may be fed directly into a mixing circuit together with sounds from a microphone or other source.

The gain control can be adjusted to produce one or more echoes. As the gain is increased the number of echoes will be increased until at a certain level the echoes become continuous and will build up into a tremendous noise. Some fascinating 'journey-into-space sounds' can be produced by allowing the echo to build up before cutting the sound off with the gain control. A little practice may be required in order to get the right balance between the microphone signal and the echo signal, but briefly the system operates as follows:

> *A sound from the microphone goes through the recording amplifier and on to the tape. The same sound is picked up a fraction of a second later by the additional head, re-amplified to its*

Electronic Sound Sources and Tone Shaping

original strength, or nearly so, and passed back on to the tape again. The sound has now been recorded twice, the second take being slightly weaker than the first or original recording, providing, of course, the gain control is set correctly. The second signal is now picked up by the extra head, and passed back round the amplifier on to the tape again. Number three 'echo' is now recorded, slightly weaker than number two.

The process continues ad lib., the sound becoming weaker on each return until it disappears altogether. If the gain control is set to a low level only one or two echoes will be generated as the return signal will very quickly fade out. If the control is set fairly high, the return signal will become strengthened and the echoes will build up into reverberating noise, which can be instantly cut off by turning the gain control quickly to zero.

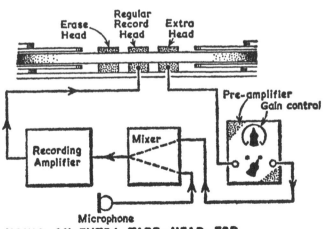

USING AN EXTRA TAPE-HEAD FOR PRODUCING ECHO'S   FIG.31

With a tape deck that lends itself to being fitted with a record/playback head *before* the erase head, as shown in Fig. 32, it becomes possible to set up a system for multiple recording. The extra head No. 1 (as in Fig. 32) is used to pick up the first recording made via the regular head (No. 2). This recording must be pre-amplified ready for mixing with the second part so that both

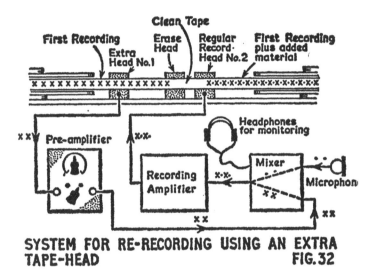

SYSTEM FOR RE-RECORDING USING AN EXTRA TAPE-HEAD   FIG. 32

are ready for re-recording. In the meantime the first recording must be erased before it reaches head No. 2, so leaving the tape clean for the re-recording. It is necessary to monitor both signals whilst the re-recording is being carried out, in order to keep in time with the original. If a practice run is required, it will be necessary to switch off the erase and record bias and switch head No. 2 out of circuit.

Perhaps this may seem a little ambitious, but those

Electronic Sound Sources and Tone Shaping

with a knowledge of recording may find it interesting and perhaps possible to use with existing equipment. These simple recording techniques open up many possibilities for amateur production of Musique Concrète and electronic music.

(The photograph of Fig. 33 shows the layout of the special recording deck used by the author for multiple recording and the production of electronic music and Musique Concrète.)

MULTIPLE RECORDING

Although not strictly electronic music, a method of adapting regular musical instruments must be mentioned, for this offers yet another means of producing something different. The following arrangement was used by the author and required a piano, two microphones, and a sine-wave oscillator for producing a vibrato effect on one of the microphone amplifiers. The microphones were fitted *inside* the piano so as to exclude room echo. One microphone was fed directly to the recording amplifier for reproduction in the normal manner. The other microphone was fed via the amplifier with the vibrato control. The output from the vibrato-controlled amplifier was fed to the recording system via a foot-pedal-operated volume control set near the piano pedals. The system enabled the piano to be recorded with its normal tone or with vibrato effects.

Extremely fast arpeggios were produced by first recording all the notes slowly and at a slow recording speed. When the composition was finally completed and played at its intended speed the result was a duet with two rather distinctive pianos, one having an unusual vibrato effect and providing accompaniment with the other playing parts of the melody at a fantastically fast rate (Ref. 6).

It is appreciated that to produce this sort of recording one must have the necessary technical knowledge and the equipment and must be a musician as well. However, it should not be difficult to find one or two willing friends with suitable recording equipment to assist in the creation of new and unusual forms of music employing traditional musical instruments and electronics together.

SPLICING AND EDITING MAGNETIC TAPE RECORDINGS

The following notes on tape splicing may be useful to those who have no experience of this. Magnetic tape may be cut and two ends spliced together without affecting the recording or playback properties of the tape. The cut should be made with a razor blade or a pair of sharp scissors. (Neither must be magnetised or allowed to come into contact with a permanent magnet, otherwise the join will produce a noise.) The 'straight splice' of Fig. 34 (A and B) is merely a straight cut through the tape. The two ends to be joined must have parallel edges and 'butt up' to each other without a gap. Cut a small piece of splicing tape and join by placing this on the '*shiny side*' of the magnetic tape. Make sure that the two pieces of tape being joined are in line with each other and on *no account* use Sellotape or similar adhesive tapes. The adhesive material gradually squeezes out and will clog up the recording head and tape guides. Use only recognised brands of splicing tape. For silent sections use white leader tape, which is convenient for

Electronic Sound Sources and Tone Shaping

writing on and can be seen when tape is running through the recorder.

The diagonal splice, Fig. 34c and D, is more frequently used for normal splicing purposes. Most tape-splicing blocks and automatic tape splicers produce this diagonal cut, which may be used instead of the straight cut.

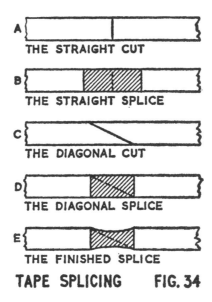

TAPE SPLICING   FIG. 34

All splices must be trimmed to prevent the edges of the splicing tape catching in the tape guides and the pressure pads (Fig. 34E). For experimental exercises untrimmed splices will do, providing they are neat and the splicing tape is cut level with the edge of the magnetic tape or leader.

CONTROLLED ATTACK AND DECAY BY TAPE CUTTING

Various forms of attack or decay to sounds can be obtained by cutting the tape at different angles, for example if a 'soft attack' is required the tape should be cut with a long angle as shown in Fig. 35A. For the

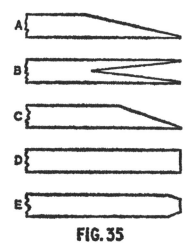

FIG. 35

CONTROLLED ATTACK OR DECAY BY TAPE CUTTING
- A. *Soft attack or decay.*
- B. *Combined attack and decay of two sounds.*
- C. *Medium attack or decay.*
- D. *Hard attack or abrupt finish.*
- E. *Softer and less abrupt than D.*

attack, the cut must lead towards the head; for the decay, the cut must lead away from the head. The cut shown as B is only suitable for full-track recording but is useful for overlapping two sounds, one with a soft attack and the other with a soft decay. The cut shown as C has about the same angle as that produced

Electronic Sound Sources and Tone Shaping

by most tape splicers and will provide a medium degree of attack or decay. The right-angled cut (D) produces a hard or abrupt beginning and ending to a sound, whilst E provides a somewhat rounder effect, not because the cut is semicircular but because the sound leads on to the head a little more gradually than the right-angled cut of D. (*Note:* These cuts were designed for full-track recordings but with care can be adapted to produce similar forms of attack or decay on half-track recordings.) It is usual to make the cut lead on to, or come away from, a short piece of leader tape which is followed by the next sound; this will isolate the sound and make the attack or decay more prominent. With care, it is also possible to splice an additional sound into the tape in parallel to one already recorded, that is, a longwise splice. This is, however, rather difficult with half-track recording.

PART THREE

The Composition of Electronic Music and Musique Concrète

The Composition of Electronic Music and Musique Concrète

The primary difference between electronic and traditional music composition is that the former cannot be performed in public by the musician(s). The process of transforming sounds by cutting and splicing, retarding, accelerating or reversing magnetic tape excludes this possibility and leads to a different procedure.

The composite sounds which are required by the composer at a given moment in a score, e.g. a melody from the sine-wave generator, an accompanying simulated pianoforte figure, together with superimposed rhythmic figures from electronic drums or cymbals, may be each produced and transformed separately in the process of recording (Ref. 1).

In the Philips *Cain and Abel* ballet the recordings were put together with the aid of several recorders and checking aids such as metronomes, etc., until finally the whole work was transcribed on to a master tape, from which discs or copy tapes could be made. As there are few musicians who can 'play' electronic apparatus and even fewer able to compose for electronic music, there is ample opportunity for original and interpretative creation. Composers of electronic music cannot normally identify their work with magnetic tape and must set down the musical thought they wish to express but in doing so must necessarily create new musical signs and notations. The scope for interpretation appears in the fact that in making, as well as putting together, the 'acoustic' layers indicated in the score there are other numerous details, such as the question of relative sound intensities, that must be decided.

The composer of electronic music has little need to offer a justification of his work. He can regard this as an experiment in an unexplored field and can supply musical motive by pointing to the fascination of creating new sounds (Ref. 8).

Most of the numerous sounds, tones and effects that can be applied in the composition and production of electronic music are shown in Table 1 (Appendix). To this may be added the multi-channel 'stereophonic' effect which provides a new dimension and a new medium for creation and interpretation. Sound can be made to emanate from points where there is no actual sound source, as well as to move in two or more directions simultaneously. This effect was used in the *Electronic Poem* at the Brussels World Fair in 1958, and those fortunate enough to hear it will support claims that the result was somewhat overwhelming.

The production of this work involved a specially equipped studio, the final composition being character-

Fig. 33. The special tape recording deck used by the author for Electronic Music and Musique Concrète.
Fig. 36. Part of the electronic and recording equipment used by the author.

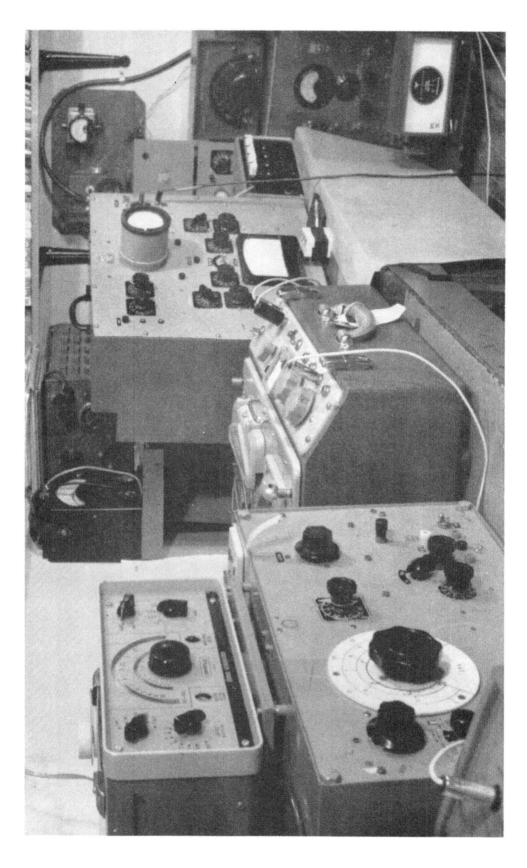

Fig. 38. *Electronic Music at the Centre of Sound, London.*

The author demonstrates the elements of Electronic Music in the Theatre at London's Centre of Sound, Archer Street, W.1, the headquarters of the exclusive British Recording Club. The Centre of Sound caters for every aspect of sound reproduction and it is the meeting place for all interested in recording, music, film and television techniques.

The Composition of Electronic Music and Musique Concrète

ised by an extraordinary wealth of sounds, the realisation of which involved considerable difficulties, e.g. deficiency of a suitable 'language' in this field; the lack of words to express what was intended and so on. Varêse, the composer, frequently indicated his wishes by explaining to the recording engineers that he wanted his expressions 'more nasal', 'less biting' or 'more rasping', and to define the necessary operations resort had to be made to onomatopoeic words such as 'wow-wow', 'poo-whip', 'tick-tock' and 'choo-char', etc. It should be mentioned that the recording was not confined entirely to electronically produced sounds but included 'concrète' sounds picked up by a microphone, e.g. piano chords, bell chimes, choral and solo singing, drum beats and workshop noises; which after electrical treatment and filtering were recorded on tape (Ref. 3).

It is not possible to give instruction on actual composition, for there are as yet no rules, neither is there any specific form of notation in which electronic music can be scored. The writer was privileged to work with the Italian composer and conductor Bruno Maderna at the Dartington Summer School of Music. He explained to students that they should not attach too much importance to the construction of sounds; it did not matter whether the sounds were beautiful or ugly. The scenery of the countryside is still beautiful even when it is raining; one can see the beauty through the rain. Maderna works, as do many other composers of electronic music, by first building up an 'orchestra' of new sounds on magnetic tape; after all, no composer can create music unless he is familiar with the sounds and range of the instruments he is scoring for. He must know what sounds are available. The composer of music for traditional instruments works on this knowledge and his training in music theory.

The composer of electronic music must first create his sounds before he can decide which he will use and how they shall be arranged but he has a far greater, in fact almost infinite range at his command.

Once the sounds and effects have been chosen, the composition can be roughly planned. Often a collection of new sounds will themselves suggest a theme for composition. The writer's own creation *The Butterfly* was conceived in this way. The sounds had to be created before the composition could be assembled to provide a phonic description of the short life-span of a butterfly. The composition won first prize in a national competition and comprised a rhythmic background with a flight sequence simulated by arpeggios on related diminished and minor chords produced from electronic sounds. Twelve different 'pitch' related speeds were used during recording, together with artificial reverberation and transformation by tape manipulation. Some of the equipment used for this recording is shown in the photograph of Fig. 36.

THE WITCHES' KITCHEN OF MUSIC

This rather apt title was used by a German writer who described the composition and performance of an opera (electronic) by the Swedish composer Karl-Berger Blomdahl. The opera is called *Aniara*, the name of a space ship in which the story takes place. Blomdahl tries to describe by electronic music the end of our planet and the dying of the last people, who happen to be in the space ship.

Blomdahl set himself the task of expressing a horrible

The Composition of Electronic Music and Musique Concrète 67

vision of the end of mankind which he accomplished with electronic music, for he decided that when the drama of mankind becomes serious the musical instruments with which we are familiar cannot provide the right expression. The new timbre and sound complexes that can be produced by electronic manipulation were brought into action. In some cases 'concrète' sounds were used together with those produced electronically. The intermezzi of *Aniara* recorded on tape and transmitted over a loudspeaker also included voice recordings. The voices, however, were purposely rendered unintelligible and what Blomdahl aimed at was Babylonian confusion of tongue. This he achieved by using the voices of famous politicians as an acoustic montage. Electronics offer unique methods for doing this and it is amazing how very much the character of a voice can be changed by electronic means. A speaker with a sonorous, quiet voice can become an excitable, nervous man. The soothing intonation of a voice in the middle pitch can take on a threatening deepness or shrill height; even the swiftness of speech can be changed to a certain extent by using a 'Springer' machine.* This is applicable to musical presentation as well as speech. These accelerations and retardations, and changes in character or timbre, sometimes sound superhuman and many of the electronic sound manipulations give almost an impression of the Apocalypse.

The German composer Karl Heinz Stockhausen used these electronic transformations for a scriptural story. He set to electronic music a passage out of the third book of Daniel, the *Gesang der Junglinge am feuerofen* (Shadrach, Meshach and Abednego cast into a fiery

* The Springer machine alters the speed without affecting pitch.

furnace). There are also singing voices to be heard, but the voices are so altered by electrical acoustic means that they are mostly no longer reognisable. Indeed, the composer was above all concerned with producing the most alarming sound effects. In a few places, only is the singing voice quite distinct.

Another composer, Ernst Krenek, has also used a scriptural subject for electronic music. He created an oratorio composed of different electronic tones, timbres and sounds and, in addition, two singing voices and the speaking voice of the composer himself. (These effects can be heard in the recording *Intelligentiae Sanctus, Pfingstoratorium für Singatimmen und Elektronische Klange*, by Ernst Krenek, DG16134, by Deutsche Gramophon.)

Reference was made to the 'Babylonian confusion of tongues' in the opera *Aniara*. The composers of electronic music seem attracted to this subject by some magic power. This is not so astonishing as it would seem, for those who are prepared to give up the conventional musical parlance and the musical grammar find themselves confronted with a vast range of tonal possibilities that the human mind can hardly realise. Our present and accepted tone system is by no means the only possible one; the majority agreed on it in order to understand the composers, who use the system and the musical language that goes with it. With electronic music, one is inclined to experience some confusion, for it is possible to lose orientation in this tremendous, unexplored and unusual sound world.

THE COMPOSITION OF MUSIQUE CONCRÈTE
The techniques employed for the composition and production of Musique Concrète are similar to those used

The Composition of Electronic Music and Musique Concrète

for electronic music; but what is Musique Concrète? The composer works in the same way as the contemporary artist, taking as his point of departure from convention, the 'sound objects' which are the equivalent of the artist's visual image. From thereon he changes the procedure of musical composition completely. Musique Concrète is often confused with electronic music, which originated in Germany and which is concerned with the electronic manufacture of sounds built up from basic tones. Musique Concrète makes use of *real everyday sounds* which are modified by tape manipulation and electronic treatment.

Most of the earlier work in this field was carried out by a Frenchman, Pierre Schaeffer, and both he and other composers willingly made use of everyday sounds which once filtered, modulated, transposed or modified become so unrecognisable that they had to take the precaution of numbering the various pieces of tape in order to recognise them later, so great was the change from the original sound.

Electronic music composition may not be so difficult to understand since basic tones are used and accurate scaling according to accepted musical theory becomes possible.

Musique Concrète calls for entirely different techniques but may include electronically produced sounds as well as natural sounds such as those of *running machinery, bells, footsteps, thunder, trains in motion* and even *speech*. Again it is really necessary to become acquainted with Musique Concrète by listening to it before being able to compose it. There are, however, no rules, as none have yet been laid down; would-be composers, like the abstract artists, have an entirely free hand. This alone makes the whole thing so much more fascinating and there is obviously plenty of scope for originality. A Musique Concrète composition may be built up entirely from one or more everyday sounds. For example a single sound may first be recorded on tape in the conventional way, via a microphone. If the recording is replayed at a higher speed the 'pitch' becomes higher and if slowed down the 'pitch' is reduced. With several speeds or continuously variable speed the sound may be re-recorded, so that each recording has a different but related pitch.

By doubling the speed the pitch would be raised an octave, therefore providing the composer with two 'notes' an octave apart. Another sound pitched between the octave notes provides three 'notes' and so on. These can be cut from the tape and spliced together to form a simple melodic phrase.

A whole composition may consist of hundreds of pieces of tape so that the task of producing a complete work can be quite a formidable one.

With a tape recorder, one can attempt the following simple first lesson in Musique Concrète composition. This is in fact a 'five finger' exercise in magnetic tape manipulation.

Supposing we take a typical sound, say a water-tap dripping into a bowl of water with a familiar 'plink-plink'. If a recording of this is slowed down, the sound will become a 'plonk', if it is speeded up, the 'plink' will become higher pitched or, to use a descriptive word, a 'tink'. By cutting two or three 'notes' of each pitch from the tape and by splicing them together you may produce something like this: 'tink-tink-plonk-plonk-plink-tink'. This very short phrase now requires a rhythmic background which can be obtained by recording a few sounds of low pitch. Cut sections of tape containing the sounds and form them into an endless loop (Fig. 37). By careful cutting and intersplicing an excellent rhythmic background may be obtained which can be superimposed on to the melody by means of a second tape recorder.

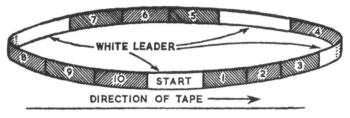

FIG. 37

CONCLUSION

Electronic music and Musique Concrète composers have differing ideas as to composition, creation and interpretation. There are conflicting opinions, too, as to whether concrete sounds only should be used or whether both electronic and concrete sounds should be combined. Some existing works are abstract in the extreme whilst others vaguely resemble music to which we are more accustomed. There is no real dividing line. The characteristic sounds of traditional musical instruments can of course be synthesised and a work composed by electronic methods. This is probably where electronic music departs from tradition, for there is little point in producing a purely synthetic version of an orchestra playing a well-known composition. The next step must therefore be an entirely new conception of 'music' with new sounds and acoustic effects. (Ref. 17.)

With conventional music the artist can choose where he wants to compose his piece of music and the performance takes place only when the composition is finished. It is carried out by musicians mostly and not by the composer himself. In electronic music the conditions are quite different. The electronic resources compel the composer to exchange his quiet room for the electronic laboratory where he has all the technical means available. Apart from this there is no distinct severance between composition and interpretation in electronic music, at least for the present. The composer must normally be assisted by an engineer, for unless he has a profound knowledge of electronics and the instruments he wishes to employ he cannot use his new 'orchestra'. This is partly due to the fact that there is no generally accepted notation for electronic music, moreover the conversion of sounds, the cutting, the acceleration and changing of recording tapes make an independent interpretation practically impossible. The various combinations are produced and converted separately and recorded on tape. They form respectively a so-called 'acoustic layer' and only in the last phase of the composition can several layers be put one upon the other as required and welded together. A tape on to which the whole of the composition has been recorded is the final result of this process.

Most of the foregoing paragraphs have been directed towards the composition of electronic music and Musique Concrète. Fairly simple equipment based on special circuits used by the author and others has been described. Considerably more technical information, outside the scope of this book, but closely connected with the subject of electronic music and Musique Concrète will be found in the books and articles that have been quoted

The Composition of Electronic Music and Musique Concrète

as works of reference. The articles by Miss Daphne Oram, for example, are enlightening, for she has produced electronic music for a number of sound and television programmes.

Finally, a note on the different trends of composition that can be distinguished. They invariably use 'electronic' means, and in particular magnetic recording, for transferring the sounds and moulding them into something new and unique. All the trends can be referred to by the collective term 'electronic music', although other definitions are used, for example: Schaeffer, in France, wants composer material to be derived from 'concrete' sounds and declares all traditional musical conventions taboo. The Studio des Kolner Rundfunks', where Eimert and Stockhausen are at work, wants to admit only synthetic sounds, produced electronically. This school of thought also seeks to avoid traditional musical elements such as melody rhythm and harmony and favours the twelve-note technique introduced by Schönberg in about 1924.

Among the composers active in this field in other countries may be mentioned Varêse, Luennig and Ussachewsky in the U.S.A., Maderna and Berio in Italy and Badings and De Leeuw in the Netherlands. Some of these composers have a less dogmatic attitude since they sometimes use electronic means in combination with, or complementary to, traditional musical instruments.

It is hoped, however, that the techniques described in this book will provide the reader with sufficient material to at least carry out a few experiments in this unexplored world of sound and music.

Stereophonic recording is now well established and in

itself should open up even wider fields for experimentation in two, or even three, dimensional forms of reproduction.

This departure from conventional music may be frowned upon by some, but justification still lies in the fascination of achieving something new and in exploring new territory.

APPENDIX

TABLE 1. ELECTRONIC TREATMENT AND SOUND SOURCES

Electronic Sound Sources

1. Sine-wave Generator.
2. Multi-vibrator (Square-wave generator).
3. White noise generator.
4. Electronic musical instruments of special design played conventionally or with mechanical damping, muting and artificial vibrato effects.

Treatment

a. Keyed or variable-pitch tones and bell effects by use of 'gating' circuits.
b. Continuously variable or keyed tones.
c. Tone shaping with electrical filters.
d. Inter-modulation between tones of different frequencies (beat notes).
e. Modulation of high-frequency tones with low-frequency tones.
f. Applied electronic vibrato effects, keyed or used in conjunction with gating circuits.
(Further treatment by tape manipulation see below.)

Concrete Sound Sources

Any sound picked up by a microphone.

Treatment

a. Removal of attack by a 'gating' circuit or by tape cutting after recording.
b. Re-recorded at various speeds to raise or lower pitch to varying degrees of the chromatic scale.
c. Removal of decay part of the sound by 'gating' circuits or tape manipulation.
d. Reversal of the sound by tape manipulation or inversion by special electronic circuits.

e. Inter-modulation and modulation of different sounds.
   f. Artificial echo.
   (Further treatment by tape manipulation, see below.)

Magnetic Tape Manipulation

Normal recording process.
Monaural (single channel).
Stereo (two or more channels to create movement of sounds).

Treatment

   a. Tape retarded (slower speeds).
   b. Tape accelerated (faster speeds).
   c. Tape speed increased or decreased gradually.
   d. Deletion of attack or decay by tape cutting.
   e. Reverse tape recording or replaying.
   f. Feedback and reverberation (echoes) by use of one or more playback heads. Diminishing echo. Echo building up to crescendo, pre-echo.
   g. Multiple recording and mixing of sounds from several tapes, or from one half-track to the other or by superimposing.

TABLE 2
The frequencies of each note of the chromatic scale in octave progression.

C	C♯	D	D♯
16·351	17·323	18·354	19·445
32·703	34·647	36·708	38·890
65·406	69·295	73·416	77·781
130·812	138·591	146·832	155·563
261·625	277·182	293·664	311·126
523·251	554·365	587·329	622·253
1046·502	1108·730	1174·059	1244·507
2093·004	2217·460	2344·318	2489·014
4168·008	4434·920	4698·636	4978·028
8372·016	8869·840	9397·272	9956·056

E	F	F♯	G
20·601	21·826	23·124	24·499
41·203	43·653	46·249	48·999
82·406	87·307	92·498	97·998
164·813	174·614	184·997	195·997
329·627	349·228	369·994	391·995
659·255	698·456	739·988	783·991
1318·510	1396·912	1479·976	1567·982
2637·020	2793·824	2959·952	3135·964
5274·040	5587·648	5919·904	6270·928
10548·080	11175·296	11839·808	12541·856

G♯	A	A♯	B
25·956	27·500	29·135	30·867
51·913	55·000	58·700	61·735
103·826	110·000	116·540	123·470
207·652	220·000	233·081	246·941
415·304	440·000	466·163	493·883
830·609	880·000	932·327	987·766
1661·218	1760·000	1864·654	1975·532
3322·436	3520·000	3729·308	3951·064
6644·872	7040·000	7458·616	7902·128
13289·744	14080·000	14917·232	15804·256

Appendix

SUITABLE COMPONENTS AND VALVES FOR USE IN THE CIRCUITS DESCRIBED

Valves

For multi-vibrator circuits, double triodes such as the Mullard ECC83, Brimar 6SN7.

Noise generator, Fig. 17, Mullard EF91.

Automatic Bell-gate, Fig. 18, V1 and V2 Mullard EF91.

Controlled Bell-gate circuit, Fig. 19, Half double triode ECC81, EF91 (Mullard) strapped as triode.

Drums and Gongs circuit, Fig. 20, Mullard EF86 or similar low-noise audio amplifier.

Circuit for simple electronic tone generator, Fig. 18, Mullard ECC81, Brimar 6SN7.

Resistors

Quarter-watt rating, 20 per cent tolerance, should be suitable for all circuits.

Potentiometers (VR)

Quarter-watt rating suitable for all circuits.

Capacitors

Paper types, coupling and de-coupling (0·001 to 0·5 mfd.), 350 v. wkg.

Electrolytics—up to 50 mfd, for cathode by-pass, 25 v. working.

Electrolytics—8 and 16 mfd, for h.t. de-coupling, 350 v. working.

Special Components

Noise generator Fig. 17, R.F. choke, Denco Limited.
Trimmer capacitor, 10–30 pfd, Philips Limited.

Switches
(Toggle and multi-way)

Fig. 18. Fig. 19, etc. Bulgin and Company Limited.

Appendix

REFERENCES

1. PHILIPS TECHNICAL REVIEW, VOL. 19, 1957/58, No. 6.
2. THE ELECTRONIC MUSICAL INSTRUMENT MANUAL. Alan Douglas, M.I.R.E. *Pitman and Sons Limited*
3. THE PHILIPS PAVILION at the 1958 Brussels World Fair (reprints *Philips Technical Review, Col. 20 Nos. 1, 2 and 3*)
4. PRINCIPLES OF ELECTRONICS. H. Buckingham, Ph.D., M.Sc., A.M.I.E.E., and E. M. Price, M.Sc. (Tech.), A.M.I.E.E. *Cleaver Hume*
5. MUSICAL ELECTRONICS WITH A HAWAIIAN GUITAR. G. F. Webster. *The Radio Constructor, Vol. 10, No. 1, August* 1956.
6. EFFECTS WITH A TAPE RECORDER. F. C. Judd, A.Inst.E. *The Radio Constructor, June/July* 1956.
7. FROM MICROPHONE TO EAR. G. Slot. *Philips Technical Library Series*
8. MUSIQUE CONCRÈTE. F. C. Judd, A.Inst.E. *Stereo Sound Magazine, August* 1959
9. PRODUCING ECHOES WITH A TAPE RECORDER. F. C. Judd, A.Inst.E. *Amateur Tape Recording Magazine, July* 1960
10. MAKING MUSIQUE CONCRÈTE. Daphne Oram. *Hi Fi News, April* 1958
11. HOW TO MAKE NEW MUSIC. Daphne Oram. *The Tape Recorder, June* 1959
12. MANIPULATION OF SIGNALS FOR MUSIC CONCRÈTE. F. C. Judd, A.Inst.E. *Tape Recording Magazine 27th January,* 1960
13. HOW TO SPLICE TAPE. I. W. Jarman *Miles Henslow Publications Limited*

Appendix

ADDITIONAL NOTES AND INFORMATION

1. Score for Electronic Music

There is at least one written score for electronic music. This is a composition by Eimert and is published in this country by Universal Editions Limited. The composition is called *Essay* and consists of eight parts for which eight different materials are defined with regard to time, frequency and elementary timbre. Instructions are included for transformation of the material—Ring modulation—Transposition —Filtering—Reverberation—Intensity Evolution, etc. The composition is based on sequences of the duration of the separate materials and the frequencies of pure tones, noise and impulse elements which are the ingredients of *Essay*.

2. Recordings of Electronic Music

Works of continental composers. Three L.P. discs issued by Deutsche Gramophon Limited:

    DG.16,132 *Introduction and Studies*. Eimert
    DG.16,133 *Studies 1 and 2*. Stockhausen
    DG.16,134 *Whitsuntide Oration*. Krenek

3. Ref. 15

Experiment in Sound by F. C. Judd, A.Inst.E. (contains examples of electronic music and Musique Concrète and demonstrates some of the techniques employed).

Issued as a pre-recorded tape by Bi-Tapes Limited, 78 Upper Berkeley Street, London, W.1.

The Power of Music, by F. C. Judd, A.Inst.E. (An electronic music composition based on a poem by John Dryden issued as a pre-recorded tape by Bi-Tapes Limited, 78 Upper Berkeley Street, London, W.1.

4. Ref. 14

Pre-recorded filtered 'white noise', suitable for electronic music composition. Twenty-five one-third octave bands of filtered white noise, 40–10,000 c.p.s. ($7\frac{1}{2}$ i.p.s.), available from Tutchings Electronics Limited, 14 Rook Hill Road, Christchurch, Hants.

5. Ref. 16
'How to make Modern Music with a Tape Recorder' by F. C. Judd, A.Inst.E. A series of articles describing simple composition and techniques for producing electronic music and Musique Concrète. *Amateur Tape Recording Magazine*— Parts 1 to 5. November, December 1960, January, February and March 1961.

6. Electronic Music Instruction for Students
The Dartington Summer School of Music held annually at Dartington Hall, near Totnes, Devonshire.

The Rose Bruford College of Dramatics, Lamorby Park, near Sidcup, Kent. Instruction is given during the annual tape recording course.

7. Survey and History of Electronic Music
Musica ex Machine, by F. K. Prieberg, published in Germany by Ullstren-Verlag.

8. Ref. 17
die Reihe & Electronic Music. Devoted to developments in Electronic Music. Published by Universal Editions Ltd.

INDEX

Index

		PAGE
A.	Additional Notes	85
	Amplifier for a tape head	50
	Analysis of Sound Waves	19
	Artificial Reverberation	48
	Attack and Decay Control	37, 58
B.	Beat Notes	23
	Bell Gate (Automatic)	38
	Bell Gate (Controlled)	39
	Buffer Amplifier and Tone Shaping Network	35
C.	Chromatic Scale v. frequency (Table 2)	79
	Circuit for Tone Production	32
	CIRCUITS	
	Gating (automatic bellgate)	38
	Gating (controlled bellgate)	39
	Phase Shift Oscillator	25

CIRCUITS—*continued*
  Tone Shaping 34
  Multi-vibrator 32
  Electronic Tone Source 33
  Buffer amplifier and tone shaping network . 35
  Noise Generator 35
  Cathode Follower 34
  Differentiating Circuit 34
  Integrating Circuit 34
  Drums and Gongs 39
  Control Unit for Electric Guitar . . 43
  Tone Control (Passive network). . . 46
  Ring Modulator 49
  Pre-Amplifier for Tape Head . . . 51
Components for Electronic Circuits (appendix) . 81
Composers work, Electronic Music . . 18, 27, 63
Composers work, Musique Concrète . . . 68
Composition of Electronic Music . . . 61
Composition of Musique Concrète . . . 68
Construction of a magnetic pick-up . . . 41
Control of Attack and Decay . . . 37, 58
Crystal pick-ups 28, 44

D. Decay Control 37, 58
  Differentiating Circuit 34
  Drums and Gongs 39

E. Echoes 52
  Editing Tape 56
  Electronic Circuits components . . . 81
  Electronic Music—Composers work . 18, 27, 63
  Electronic Reproduction 16
  Electronic Sound Sources, hybrid . . . 18
  Electronic Tone Source 33
  Electronic Treatment and Sound Sources (Table 1) 77, 78
  Electronic Vibraphone 45
  ELEMENTS OF ELECTRONIC MUSIC . . . 15

F. Formation of Sound Waves 22
  Frequency v. Chromatic Scale (Table 2) . . 79

Index

G.	Gating Circuits	37
	General references (appendix)	83
	Generator (Sine Wave)	17
	Guitar (Hawaiian)	42
	Guitar (Plectrum)	41
H.	Harmonics	21
	Hawaiia Electric Guitar	42
	Head Pre-amplifier	50
	Hybrid Electronic Sound Sources	18
I.	Instruction for Students (appendix)	86
	Integrating Circuit	34
L.	Loops, Tape	71
M.	Magnetic Pick-ups	28, 41
	Magnetic Tape	16
	Modulation, Ring	16, 45
	Monitoring a Recording	52
	Multiple Recording	55
	Multi-vibrator, The	18
	Multi-vibrator as a tone source	31
	Musique Concrète, Composers Work	68
	Musique Concrète, Composition	68
N.	Network for Tone Correction	45
	Noise Generator	18, 36
	Noise—White	18, 37
O.	Optical Siren	19
	Oscillator, phase shift	25
	Oscillator, Sine Wave	36
	Oscillator, Square Wave	18
P.	Passive Tone Control Network	46
	Phase Shift Oscillator	25
	Pick-ups, Crystal	28, 44
	Pick-ups, Magnetic	28, 41
	Plectrum, Electric Guitar	41

	Poemè Electronique	27
	Pre-amplifier for a tape head	50
	Producing Electrical Tones . . .	25, 32
R.	Reference (appendix)	83
	Re-recording systems	54
	Reverberation, Artificial echo	48
	Ring Modulation	16
	Ring Modulator	45
S.	Sine Waves	20
	Sine Wave Generator	17
	Simple Recording Techniques	48
	Siren, Optical	19
	Sound Waves, analysis	20
	Sound Sources	17
	Splicing and Editing Tape	56
	Stereophony	27
	Students, Instruction courses (appendix) . .	86
T.	Tape Editing	56
	Tape Head pre-amplifier	50
	Tape Loops	71
	Tape Splicing	57
	Tone Correction Network	45
	Tone Shaping	34
	Treatment and Sound Sources (Table 1) .	77, 78
	Trends in Composition	73
V.	Vibraphone, Electronic	45
	Vibrato	24
	Vibrato Oscillator	25, 33
W.	White Noise	18, 37
	Witches Kitchen of Music	66

Lightning Source UK Ltd.
Milton Keynes UK
UKOW06f0001290415

250495UK00005B/75/P